Soul Notes Poetry by Em

Published by Marginal Pul

Marginal Publishing House, Suite 3.3, Tempest Building, L2 2DT.

www.marginalpublishing.co.uk

Cover and illustrations by Ella Fradgley.

ISBN: 978-1-9164448-8-1

Printed in the United Kingdom.

1st Print Edition.

MARGINAL

Marginal is a revolution in publishing, founded by Comics Youth in 2019. Led by young people, for young people, Marginal is the first youth-led publisher of its kind in the UK. With it, we hope to not just change the landscape of young people's reading in the UK, we also strive to use Marginal as a platform with which to nurture marginalised talent and express a diverse set of voices and experiences which are currently going unheard. Marginal aims to publish a diverse collection of books which reflect the full diaspora of identities, backgrounds, experiences, and perspectives of marginalised young people.

Marginal seeks to give agency to young people in developing narratives that reflect their identities and experiences. In doing so we want to raise the self-esteem of young creators while inspiring them to become a positive point of influence for other marginalised young creators to do the same.

We're committed to publishing stories that platform the untold and the underrepresented. As such, we're especially committed to working with marginalised young people across the Liverpool City Region with voices that are currently underrepresented in print media.

These include young people from LGBTQIA+ and BAME communities, looked after young people and those who experienced inequality, young people from working class backgrounds and young people experiencing mental ill-health, special education needs and beyond.

Emily McChrystal

Emily McChrystal is a poet, activist, a full-time over-thinker and the Youth Empowerment Director of Comics Youth CIC-which works with marginalised youth to use creative outlets to navigate complex experiences. Emily is the first person to be published by Marginal' with her debut poetry book, 'Soul Notes Poetry'. She lives in Liverpool and occupied the box room in her Mum's house whilst making this very book! She remains a full-time over-thinker.

Ella Fradgley

Ella Fradgley is a working class creative and full-time romantic whose rose-tinted illustrations fill the pages of 'Soul Notes Poetry'. Ella is a passionate activist and Co-Creative Director of 'Where are the Girlbands', a social justice initiative that aims to celebrate and create safe spaces for musicians of marginalised genders. With a degree in Fine Art from Manchester School of Art, her creative practice is focussed on themes of healing and radical love. This love is evident in the collaboration between Ella Fradgley and Emily McChrystal, where their friendship has created flourishing pathways for care, creativity, and enchantment.

Dedication

My parents for protecting my creativity.

My Nan and Grandad for showing me what true love looks like.

My first love for showing me that mine can look a little different.

And to You - May you always find and create spaces in which you belong.

SOUL NOTES POETRY

WRITTEN BY EMILY MCCHRYSTAL

ILLUSTRATED BY ELLA FRADGLEY

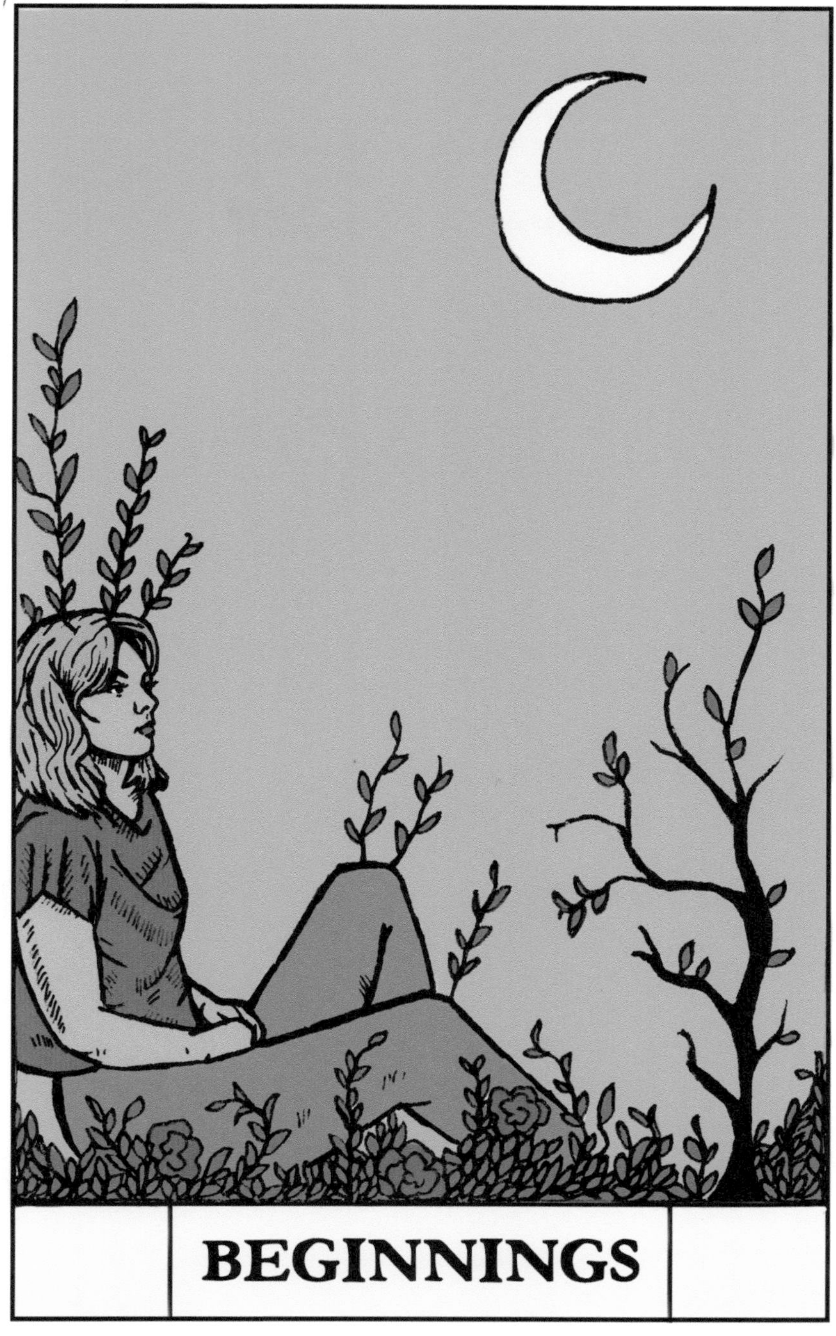

BEGINNINGS

When the moon met the sun, at dusk and
dawn, the times they could kiss in secret.

Tunnel Vision.

When your patience has run thin
And you're finding it hard to
fit in everything you need to.

And the view from the tunnel you're in
makes it impossible to see the light.

When it feels like the end,
it seems the perfect time

to begin again.

Little Red Balloon.

Tie string to your wrist,
we want to find you in the crowd.
There you go,
the Little Red Balloon.
Floating up and flying high,
we wait to see you walk on by.
We wait and we wait,
hours pass through,
but still,
no sign of you.
Tie the string to your wrist,
You let yourself fly.
The hustle and bustle,
isn't there in the clouds,
you say you can't tell if its ever a bad day,
they all seem so sunny.
I always found that funny,
How we were too busy checking the ground for you,
To realise you were tying knots in your string to the raindrops
above us.
Too busy checking to see if you'd fallen,
To realise you were sliding down sunbeams.

To the red balloon wearer,
Let yourself fly.
Even when nobody believes you can.

Advice On How To Breathe When You Don‹t Want To.

Tie one end of the string to your

                         rib cage

and the other to the smell of freshly cut grass, the stranger
that complimented you
or the memory of a time before

                      and run.

Let the string caught on your good days tug at your lungs and
force them to open up again.

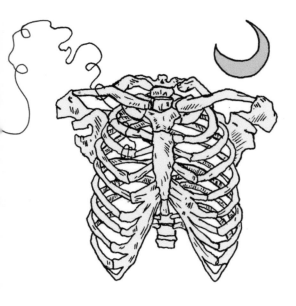

Venus wears lipstick.

"I'm gay"
says the girl with long brown softly blown hair, flowing down her
back
like the waterfall she was born in.

"Oh… so you're bi."
Her soft glow of highlight kissed by the sun,
the sun is the queen of feminine energy and she has it all on her
cheek.

"No, I'm a lesbian."
The moon once walked her home,
although no one believed her.
No one believes her.
She talks and tells but the bells of lies ring.

No one trusts a girl with lipstick on her teeth.

"You can't be" they say in a way that kicks Venus off of her chair,
she stands.
She stands tall but doesn't say anything at all, she pushes on the
chest of the lipstick toothed girl,
she says to go.

Go and go some more,
for you are the queen of raw womanhood.
Of push up bras and glitter strays.
The queen of raw womanhood.
Of foundation that doesn't match and long nails painted with
hearts.

You are the sun,
a ball of feminine energy,
A woman who holds the moon's craters on her way home from
beauty school.

A woman who loves women.
A lesbian, who wears lipstick.
A lesbian, who is made of all the women from before.

Say no more, love who you love,
love how you love.
Listen to the whispers of femme tales in the air of stories of
dresses, gowns and delicate hands to brush upon.

Love who you love,
love how you love,
live how you dare.

Finding credence amongst land.

I know the sun will rise in the morning,
I know the sun will set at night.
It is this solid faith in the universe
that I will harvest throughout life.

You do not need permission to be
hopeful, hope is yours.

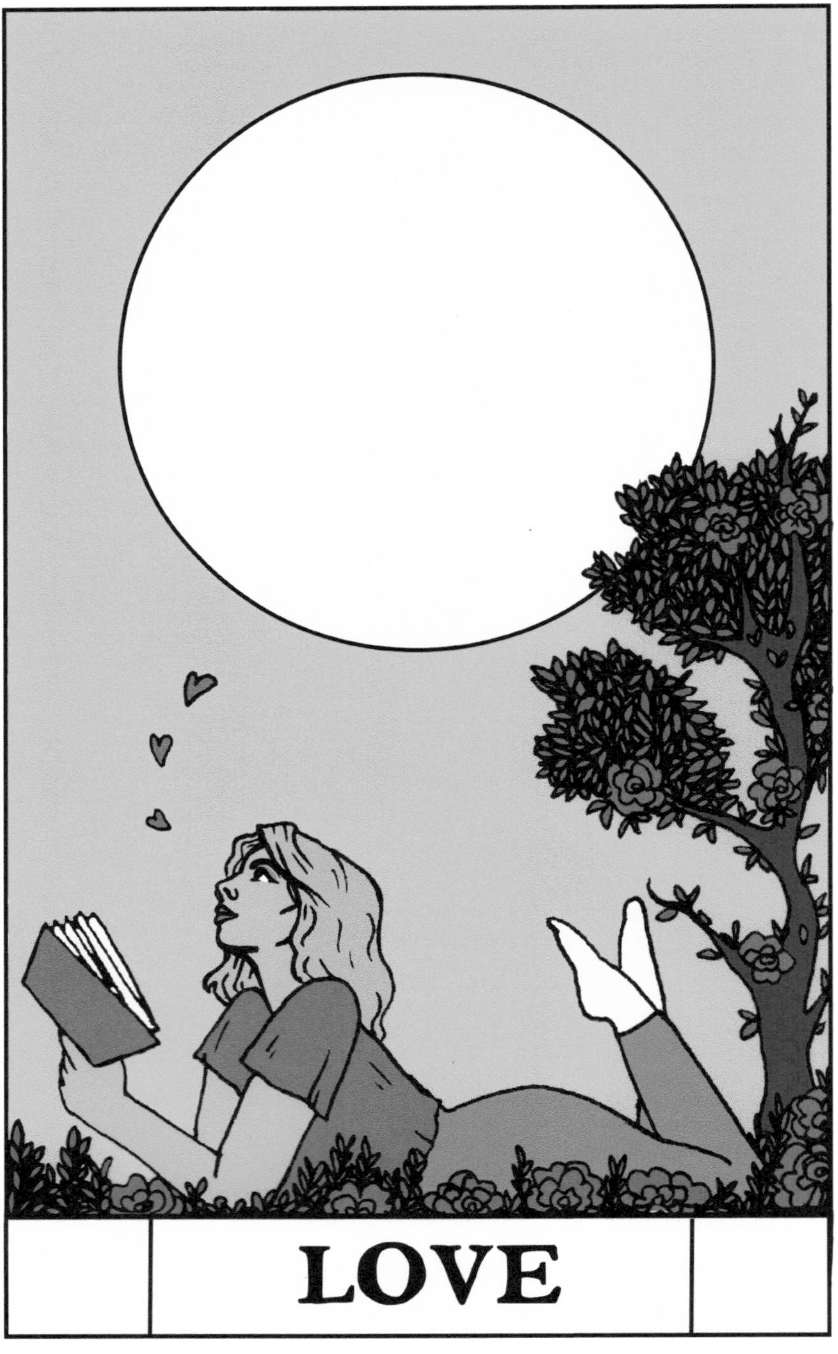

LOVE

Sweet Heart.

There she is,
dripping in raspberry tea,
bees buzzing around her for her sweetness.
How lucky I am to be the one

who wipes her sticky cheek,
to kiss the girl in the teacup
goodnight.

Your Soundtrack.

Like a record that keeps on scratching,
we run in imperfect circles.

Chapped Lips.

I have seen the best of you
and the worst of you,
I choose both.

Let's talk about your cracked lips

that you keep biting through.
I think maybe it's a way of you
trying to crawl out of yourself,
or maybe it's just a thing that you do-

I always had a habit of overanalysing.
To create the simple things into an agonising
tale of pain.
How the stains on your bed sheets are from running in your sleep.

I guess sometimes its not this deep.
I can't help but look into your eyes
and hope you realise that all you need
is right there.

Right behind your lips,
In-between your eyes,
stored inside your odd socks,
kept in a knot of your hair.

I can't help but be here with you,
and think of how much I love you.
How much I would do
to fix it all.

Remember to buy lip balm.

A Kiss So Strong.

They say the sky is the limit
but I think they forget that when we kiss,
we are tangled into the star's hair
and we interrupt the planets' paths.

They forget that we change the course of the months by making
the moon rock.

Kilonovas.

I read about love,
being a collision of the stars above,
rearranging and changing the planets
plans.

I heard about love,
making you shaky and hot,
making you question everything that
you've been taught.

I was told about love,
being messy and nervous,
confusing and tough,
I never though I would be enough for love's chaos.

But when I met love,
she wasn't like this at all.
She feels like home even when I've forgotten what home means.

When I first met love,
I could hear her say,
"Welcome home,
It's only the stars, the universe and us."

When I held love,
there was no chaos at all.
Everything shifted into place
and love had the face of comfort.

Protecting the Balance.

If you ever choose you want to dance in the rain,

just one time.

I will fold myself up and be your cane.
I will help you stand-dance-skip,
I will aid you in the rain dance.

I will aid you in the rain dance-
we can prop each other up,
we can let the rain seep into our skin,
we can absorb the drops like sunlight.

I want to be your umbrella.
But when you want to dance, we will dance.

It's All Fate.

I will meet you at our constellation,
just to the left.

                                    I will help you catch your breath
                          As we count the stars wishing for you.

                          The path you walk has two footprints,
                                    you're where you need to be.

You're here,
with me.

Stifled by love.

I always had a habit of picking the prettiest flowers,
right from their roots
and wanting to store them in a cup of water
on my windowsill.

I didn't understand that they couldn't survive there,
I didn't understand that I was killing them.

They would still droop
and die weeks after.

Climate Love.

I'll love you till the flood waters rise,
I'll die content if my last look is in your eyes.
The smoke from the burning forest fires
will make us cough until "I Love You"

sounds like a song we no longer recognise.
I'll hold your hand while the sand of the beaches
hold their last pieces of plastic
and we'll think how fantastic it was,

to walk along them back in years before.
When our feet were not sore from cuts off bottle lids,
just tender lips from kisses as shy kids
in love with the future.

Reticent.

Like a flower waiting to be picked.

My love in-between us

waiting for us to notice.

She smiles and tells me she sees it.

She knows I don't hand it to her,

that I need some time to warm up.

She says she likes the wait,

the relief of a hug after a long day,

I'm learning not to wait until she asks,

to just relax and show her.

I hand her my love,

She says thank you,

and gives me hers.

She said she's waited forever.

THE FEELINGS INBETWEEN

Universally Halfhearted.

A jigsaw with a missing piece,
a book with the last sentence scribbled out.

A lolly-ice that falls right off the stick
and a drink that's room temperature.

A hug that doesn't last long enough
and a trip to the beach while it rains.

The disappointment that is found
in places we hope for happiness.

How universal the longing for completeness is.

Things you definitely don't need in your backpack.

glass jars,
your lego collection,
the pen you stole in 2013,
love notes you never sent,
the weight of the world,
secrets stuffed right at the bottom,
that leaflet you felt too awkward to refuse,
the grief they left you alone with,
thoughts that keep you awake,
regrets (a pack of these),
empty space for anticipated sadness.

These don't belong on your shoulders,
take them out.
One by One.

Analogue's hands.

It always feels like its chasing us.
Deep and shallow shaky breaths
follow us to every milestone,
every change.

Every day that goes too fast,
the breath gets closer and closer.
Whispers of missed opportunities
screaming us awake.

Once we are out of bed,
we are running as fast as our
legs may take us without snapping
under the pressure.

Running, running out of breath.
We have to stop at some point.
But once we've stopped, it's disorienting.

The thing that's been chasing us,
is in front of us,
running away.

In our
         sleepwalking
                        sleeprunning state

we didn't realise
we were the chasers.

Grief.

It's too big, too heavy.
Its not made for a body like mine.
It just doesn't fit right.

I might try to put it back on the hanger,
stuff it into the back of the wardrobe,
not let it make my shoulders tender anymore.

I try to push it into my top drawer,
it was too big.
It spills out over onto the floor.

It tries to leak under my door.
I said it couldn't run from me.
The stitching is caught on my shoe.

I guess that's when I realised I had to wear it.
I'm not sure what it should do,
It never keeps me warm.

It has no real purpose but to make my chest heave and my
spine crinkle under the weight.
People are noticing.

A lady asks me if she can carry it for me.
She doesn't realise that it's stitched into my arms.
Attached.

I tell it, it can't run from me.
I carry it around every day,
over my now bruised, weakened build.

The pockets are filled
with memories of a time before.
The zip catches on my tears

and all my fears of the unknown
get tangled in the buttons.

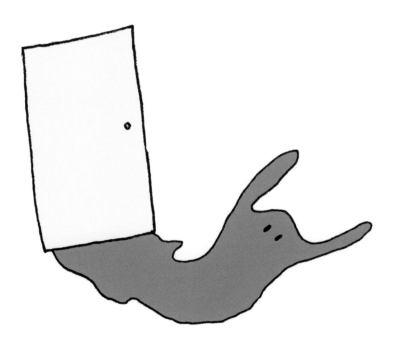

Box Room.

It's okay to stay in here
all day,
I know they say it's bad for your health
but this is the only way I feel safe.

I guess I've given so much of my heart
beyond these four walls,
I struggle to clamber out of them.
My picture frame falls.

They don't understand
that my left-hand hangs on the walls,
my heart stored in the pillowcases,
my secrets hidden in obvious spaces.

I know that I should let go,
but why would I want to know
a world outside these walls,
when these walls built themselves around me?

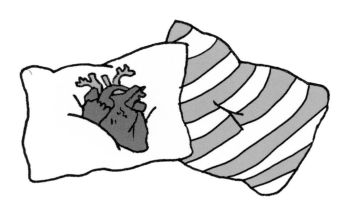

Stagnant.

Rest is my forte,
on the bad days I'd hear her say
to wake up and welcome the world,
but I'd rather stay curled up here
while I lay awake,
waiting for the day to arrive
so that I can waste it,
all over again.

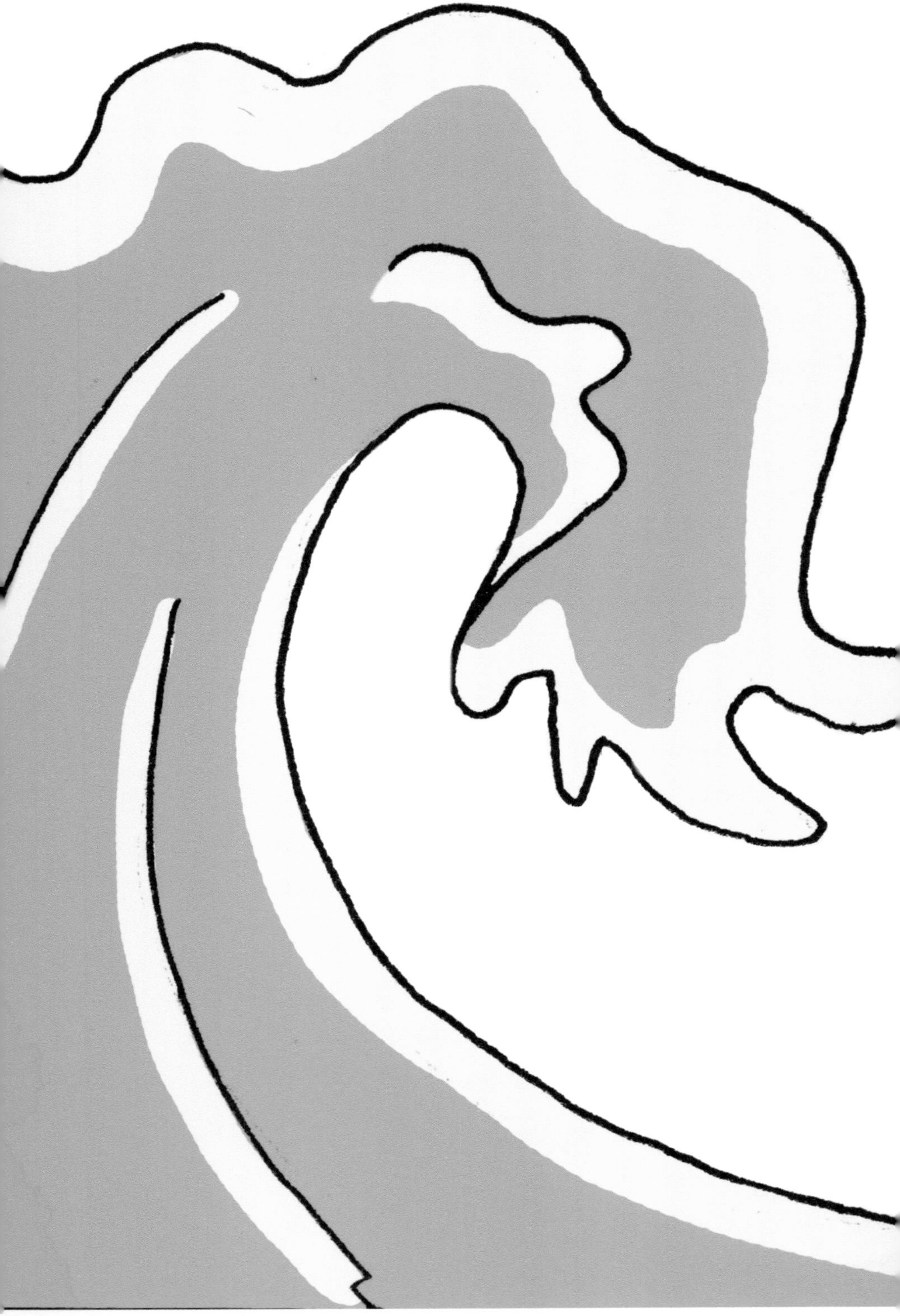

Kintsugi.

The waves always come
when we least expect them to,
when we thought the glue
used last December

was finally the best one.
But still,
the pieces fell apart   again
and I'm struggling the find the art in it.

The one where all the broken pieces
make the floor look beautiful again,
but my pieces just trip people up

and get glass in their right foot
because it's always the wrong time
to fall apart,
always so many things to do

and get done.
There's no time to shatter into   pieces.
We have no time to collect them all up
so, we leave them behind.

We brush up the left side of our brain
and forget what remained of it
when we look back in a year,
because being here isn't about remembering

It isn't about surrendering to the waves
that chip at our shoulders,
it's about getting up getting up getting up
but all I feel is fed up.

Just our luck,
to be stranded with the   chipped one,
                    the   forgotten one,
                    the   cut up right foot

with the wrong words all the time
but this is fine. It's fine.

                    We will make new pieces to replace the old
and we will make our own molds of what happiness should look like.

                    Sometimes happiness wears a frown
          while dancing in a gown sewn from a guided video on YouTube,
happiness smells like not showering for days but still remembering to
                                        paint your nails.

          The trails of happiness can be found in a sad moment,
                                        In a sad person,
                                        In a sad time.
          Wave at happiness as it passes by

Its come over to see you, to say Hi.

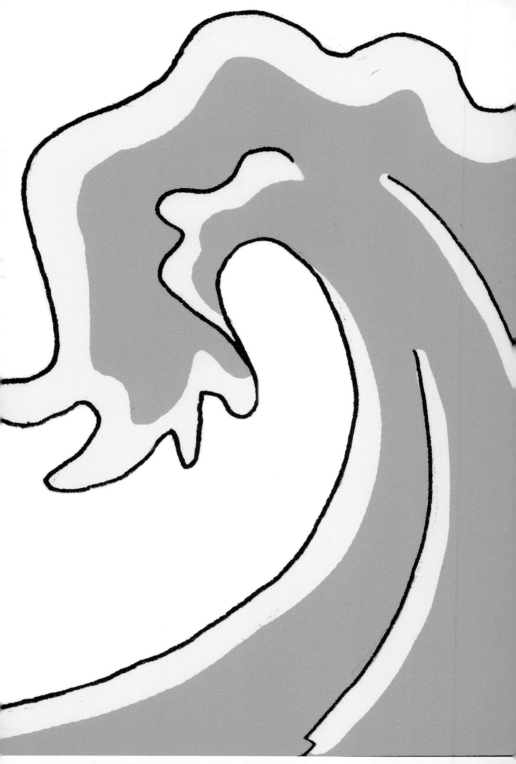

A grateful heart is a magnet for miracles.

Brain Freeze.

A heaviness that won't shift-
        In the way things should be working,
I find myself slurping this ice blast,

Brain freeze is a real thing and it's happening,
for real.
I can feel my brain shrivel up and melt away into my shoul-
ders

my doctor thinks it's my own brain
freezing up all my thoughts-
but I told him it can't be,
I had a lot of ice before I came.

It's my own fault.
My own fault for drinking it and eating it
all at once,
but when I like something,

I really like it.
So, I devoured the ice
and now its my own fault
that my brain's freezing over.

It all hangs on thinning string.

It all hangs on thinning string.
Fragility is in everything,
yet it is the thing we feel
we must shrink away,
never say we are fragile

never share the cracks
that formed from lack of love or other.
Don't share with one another
the pressure the non-shatter glass is under.

But now it's here for all to see.
The vulnerability of unavoidable fragility.
Time is so fragile that it ran away from us,
Normality is so fragile we've forgotten who it used to be.

Did normality used to see you off to work each day?
Did it show you every single way that your routine was a comfort
you don't remember forming?

The hands of time freeze up sometimes
It goes so fast you can't see the hands spinning anymore.
Impossible to tell the difference.

Normality is fragile,
time is fragile,
yet both brought a sense of unbreakable
security

that we could never see,
until it was gone or wrong or messed up.
When the world is shaking like a snow globe-
we just have to stand and watch the pieces fall over us.

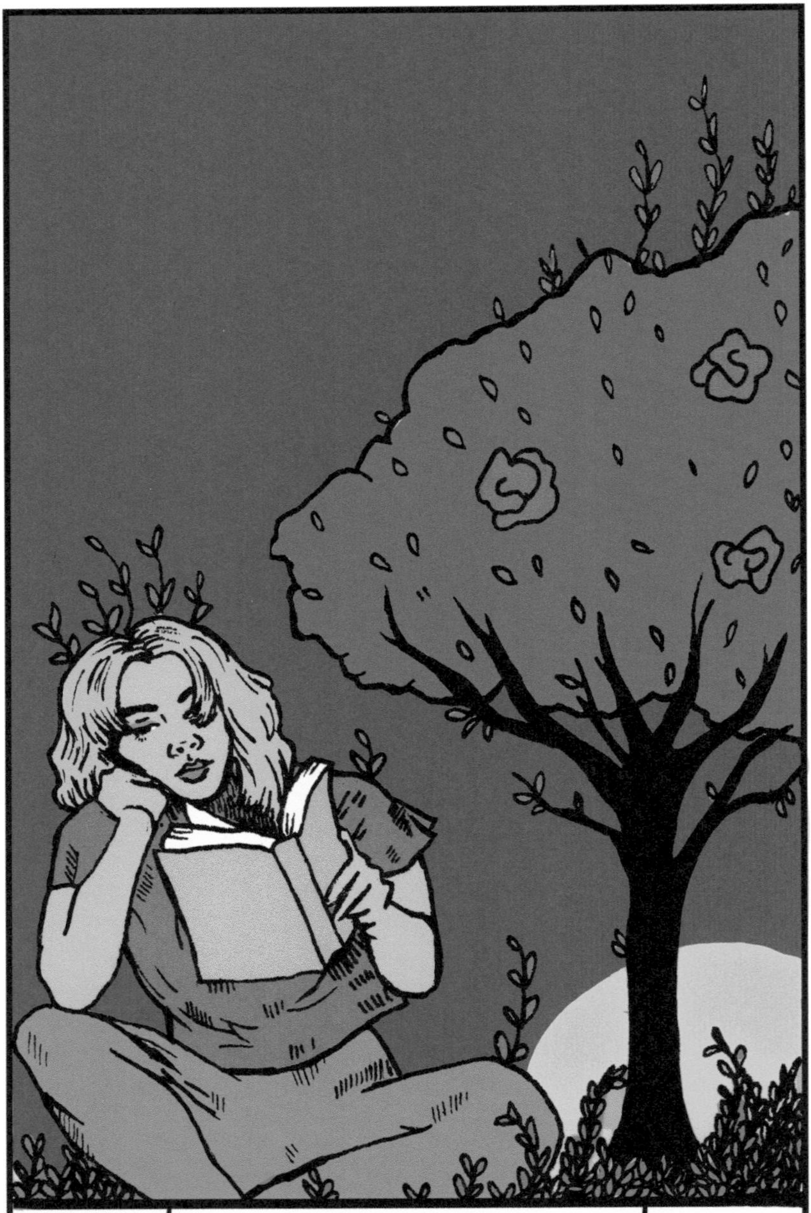

SELF

The making of a memoir.

You'd be forgiven for thinking
that the impact of you landing on this earth,
had not an impact at all.

Not even a petal on the daisies head
came away from its center.
Not a dent in the soil from where you crashed down to earth
with an ungraceful,

T H U D.

You'd be forgiven for thinking nobody noticed.
They noticed.

The daisy realised how tough it's soft petals were,
and the soil was reminded of the nutrients it harvests every
season.

You didn't destroy anything,
no trail of movements left behind.
To be remembered,
you don't need to change the foundations.

It's how you made things feel,
how you preserved the good.
You'd be forgiven for thinking no one recalls the crash

but everyone felt the shift of

You.

Perfection has no place

In shaping

You.

Paladin.

Safety is in me,
it bumps and pumps through my heart.
That is my superpower.

Mother Land.

Every time you get caught on a tree branch,
every time you trip up on that tuft of grass,
the universe is trying to pull you back

home.

Gaining More Than Weight.

Take up space,
be full and loud and visible,
be present in a room.

With strength comes growth,
with growth comes strength.
Move mountains and become them.

If mother nature can expand oceans
you can expand your home.

The Blueprint.

Everything has a plan, and you are a part of it.

You belong here.

Amongst the mess and the calm,
the good and the bad.

You are the perfect balance.

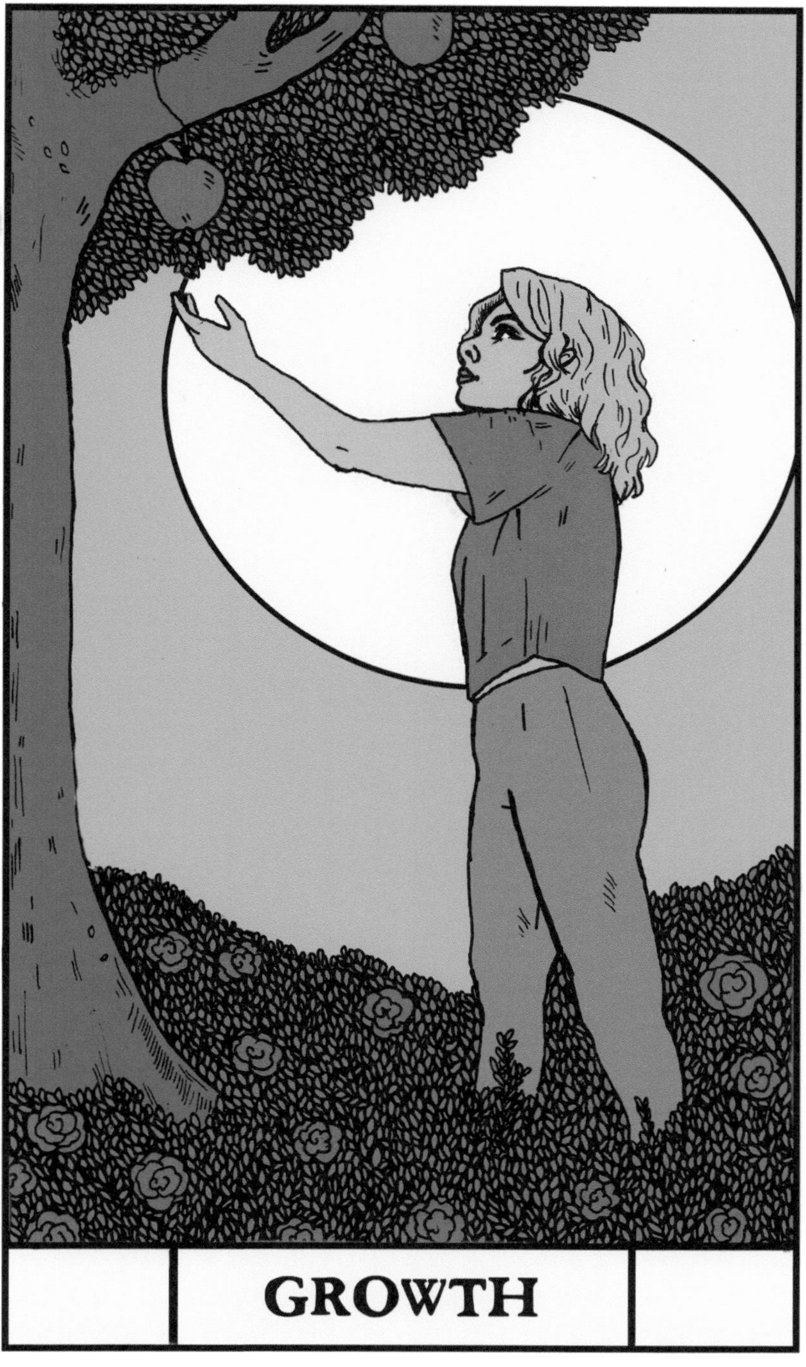

GROWTH

The Greenhouse effect.

You are your own protection,
Mother Nature's most favourite selection
of wind, sun and ice,
sunlight is hidden in your chest.

Just behind your rib cage,
wrapped in ivy from the growth of the summer before,
you are so much more than just a
shelter.

Your heart is a helter-skelter,
up from love down from fears,
but it always comes to an end.
You will ride it out.

Plant the seed of love in your stomach,
Just to the left,
the best spot for growth.
Use your own sunlight and grow.

Use your tears to water the seed of love,
use your clouds to make it resilient.
Use your gusts of power to strengthen the stem,
and let them know that you are here

here to be seen,
to be known.
To grow and never stop growing.
Keep going, you are made of the universe.

Yesterdays.

She told me this tree
reminded her of the girl she used to be.
More carefree and less worried about
what the next meal or job would be.

She told me this tree
was one she captured back in 2014.
I guess she didn't realise
what this would mean back then.

Nostalgia is a drug she loves to
love on,
she takes a hit from the scenery known all too well,
tells me of the lake she fell into

that she's now too tired to walk around.
Too busy with her clock stuck on yesterday's time

to realise that life is passing her by.
But it seems that memories fit her
like a picture she's trying to climb back into,
a tree she's trying to climb back up

without the danger of a grazed knee
and wanting to see life
from a different view.

If a branch snaps,
It's okay.
It was ready to decay and
say its goodbyes.

Feel the fresh new breeze and remember
these moments
were made for me
and the trees that touch the clouds.

The Test.

Every

      hurdle

was

placed

on

your

path

to

see

how

high

you

could

            jump,

not

how

fast

you

could

fall.

My strength looks very different now.
It is turning into something I don't recognise.

But it is

there.

Here.

Somewhere.

Fault lines.

Let's make mistakes,
let's get it all completely wrong
and wake up with knots in our hair
because the love we find on good days

will still be there
on the bad ones.

Let's make mistakes,
let's get it all completely wrong,
let's swear and stomp and make a scene

because after all,
what does anything really mean?

Let's make mistakes,
let's get it all completely wrong.
Although our list of wrongs may be long
we will find lessons in all of them.

So, let's get tucked into bed with the pillows at the wrong end
and wake up to the world from a new perspective.

Where wrongs are right
and rights are left.
And love can be found in the pockets of thieves who hand it right
back.

Long lost, me.

Looking and searching,
under the blankets of love,
here I find myself.

I HOPE ONE DAY

I'M BRAVE
ENOUGH TO BE
YOUNG